police car

bulldozer

helicopter

speedboat

ferry

airplane

sailboat

hot-air balloon

scooter

13

bus

coast guard boat

unicycle

taxi

car

ambulance

ultralight

Clothes

shoes

shirt

sneakers

glasses

bow

T-shirt

bag

necklace

sweater

shorts

pajamas

skirt

tights

dress

mittens

watch

jeans

slippers

cardigan

socks

scarf

coat

vest

woolen hat

underpants

boots

overalls

pocket

buttons

leggings

On the farm

turkey

goose

gosling

goat

kid

farmer

tractor

wheelbarrow

hay bale

vegetables

ostrich

duck

ducklings

sheep

lamb

horse

foal

tractor and plow

calf

cow

pig

piglet

chicks

hen

rooster

eggs

sheepdog

donkey

carrot

farmhouse

Family

mom

baby

dad

aunt

uncle

grandpa

grandson

grandma

grandparents

granddaughter

pet

boy

friends

toddler

brother

sister

cousins

grandchild

teenager

girl

child

pregnant

adult

parents

twins

Pets

turtle

parrot

food

hamster

pony

rabbits

chinchilla

tarantula

cage

dog

puppy

canary

ferret

guinea pig

cat

kitten

mouse

doghouse

goldfish

ball

bone

snake

iguana

basket

rat

hutch

birdcage

Dinnertime

lemon

raspberry

cheese

apple

ice cream

juice

broccoli

tomato

eggplant

potato

banana

strawberry

orange

glass

milk

onion

carrot

fork   knife

plate

pizza

mushrooms

watermelon

cake

cupcake

egg

jello

peas

pepper

pineapple

yogurt

sweet corn

grapes

Wild animals

koala

gorilla

zebra

lion

flamingo

kangaroo

shark

bear

rhinoceros

walrus

sea lion

dolphin

penguins

snake

crocodile

polar bear

hippopotamus

whale

peacock

monkey

jellyfish

elephant

tiger

cheetah

yak

panda

giraffe

Playtime

 jump rope

 book

 clown

 doll

 pencils

 guitar

 piggy bank

 teddy be

 xylophone

 drum

building blocks

 ball

 Hula-Hoop

yo-yo

 dinosaur

 train

rocking horse

tablet

slinky

dollhouse

marbles

tricycle

crown

violin

skateboard

tea set

roller skates

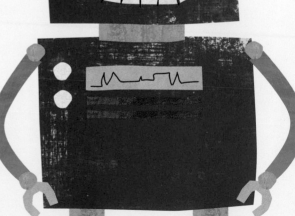

robot

space hopper

race car

In the park

bench

ladybug

flowers

bumblebee

fly

toadstool

nest

snail

slide

kite

pond

boat

moth

picnic

acorn

Frisbee

ants

bush

tree

spider

slug

ball

swing

butterfly

leaf

Bath time

toothpaste

toothbrush

hairdryer

soap

towel

hairbrush

rubber duck

shampoo

shower

sponge

bathtub

bubble

faucet

washcloth

comb

makeup

tissues

perfume

toilet paper

shower cap

mirror

toilet

bathrobe

weighing scales

sink

first-aid kit

At the beach

paddle and ball

seaweed

sunglasses

thongs

inner tube

shell

windmill

ball

sunscreen

fan

swimsuit

crab

goggles

starfish

beach bag

towel

sea horse

fish

popsicle

deck chair

sailboat

parasol

sun hat

shovel

sand castle

bucket

drink

Weather

sun

cloud

cold

rainbow

snow

rain

woolen hat

hot

snowman

mitten

scarf

winter

tornado

wind

lightning

spring

umbrella

snowflake

fall

ice

rain boots

raincoat

puddle

summer

Body

head

nose

eye

teeth

neck

arm

mouth

foot

tongue

elbow

ear

tummy

knee

leg

chin

forehead

thigh

toe

backside

hand

finger

hair

eyebrow

cheek

lips

muscle

Opposites

short

tall

fast

slow

in

out

on

off

small

big

front

back

day

night

awake

asleep

wet

dry

long

short

happy

sad

up

down

fat

thin

hot

cold

Colors, shapes, and numbers

pink dress

yellow ducklings

purple sweater

gold crown

blue jeans

green frog

silver armor

orange pumpkin

black cat

white mouse

brown owl

red apple